Just Enough Requirements and SDLC

1st Edition

Just Enough Requirements and SDLC

Requirements, Documentation, Waterfall, and Agile.

An Introduction to writing software requirements and documentation and using those in the Software Development Life Cycle.

Part of the "Just Enough" series on the practices and techniques of software development.

Ed Crookshanks
Nokel Services
Spring 2017

Cover image: Kelsey Crookshanks

ISBN-13: 978-1544257518
ISBN-10: 1544257511

Version 2017-Spring

To Amy, Noah, and Kelsey

TABLE OF CONTENTS

Preface

About the "Just Enough" Series
This series of books is aimed at programmers who are new to formal development, or those seasoned programmers who would like to gain an understanding of processes they haven't used or been exposed to. Common examples would be recent graduates or those taking some type of "Software Practicum" course; someone who is self-taught or a hobbyist and is looking to move to the corporate world; or someone who has worked in very small software organizations where development is less controlled. Although there may be statements about retail software the emphasis is mainly on enterprise software within a medium to large organization.

Each book provides a relatively brief but in-depth discussion of its topic. While I dare not say that each book "is really all you need to know" on a particular topic, I feel that the major points and most frequently used practices and techniques are discussed. There are thousands of software producing organizations out there and there is no way to even come close to discussing the fine points that each organization uses. However there are some common practices and techniques that are the same or similar in principle. My aim is to keep these topics relatively short and more at a "getting started" level than a "deep dive" into each. As someone who has interviewed many people I can attest to the fact that hearing "I'm familiar with the concept and I've worked through some examples" is much better than "I've never heard of or used that technique." At the very least during interviews I hope to enable the first answer with books in this series.

Another reason that I'm not going into extreme detail on each topic is that there are many other books with hundreds of pages that do that. I would rather introduce these topics to a level that is quickly usable, thereby letting the reader decide which to investigate further based on experience or interest. Learning, especially in IT/programming, is a life-long pursuit and while techniques usually change slower than technology both do evolve at a pace that is quicker than other engineering disciplines.

With that, I hope to keep each book in this series at under one hundred pages and group the topics so that they flow together and are complementary. Brevity will be key in that; examples will be kept simple and code will often be "snipped" to exclude items not directly being discussed.

Disclaimer

The tools and techniques discussed in this guide are not the only ones on the market. If a particular tool is mentioned in this guide it does not mean that it is the only tool for the job, is endorsed in any way by the author or publisher, or is superior in any way to any of its competitors. Nor does mention of any tool in this publication insinuate in any way that the tool owners or resellers support or endorse this work. Visual Studio® is a registered product of Microsoft and all other Microsoft product trademarks, registered products, symbols, logos, and other intellectual property is listed at http://www.microsoft.com/about/legal/en/us/IntellectualProperty/Trademarks/EN-US.aspx. All other trademarks, registered trademarks, logos, patents, and registered names are the property of their respective owner(s). We are aware of these ownership claims and respect them in the remainder of the text by capitalizing or using all caps when referring to the tool or company in the text.

Any example code is not warranted and the author cannot be held liable for any issues arising from its use. Also, the references provided for each topic are most definitely not an exhaustive list and again, their mention is not to be construed as an endorsement, nor is any resource left off the list to be considered unworthy. Many additional books, web sites, and blogs are available on these topics and should be investigated for alternate discussions. Any mentions of names anywhere in the book are works of fiction and shouldn't be associated with any real person.

Notes about Software

Examples are provided mostly in C# and different tools, all of which have some level of free software available, such as Visual Studio Community Edition. Enterprise versions of these tools may exist, or similar tools with stricter licensing models and slightly different semantics may exist; it is simply assumed that tools at the educational level will be closer to the free versions. Also, most hobby developers or recent graduates will probably make use of free tools instead of starting with an expensive development tool suite. If a particular topic/example is not given in a familiar language or with a familiar tool it should be easily translated into another environment. Where possible, notes on how different platforms solve different problems in different ways will be noted. Some of these tools may already be mandated by an employer, others may be free to choose which tools to use to start a practice discussed here.

Please note – the examples will be kept necessarily simple. In fact, most of the examples will be so short that the tools and techniques used on them will probably not seem worth it. However in the context of much larger systems, enterprise systems, these tools and techniques are very useful.

Author Summary

Ed Crookshanks has over 20 years of experience in software development. He started with C on a VAX machine for medical research, moved on to C++ on both Unix and PC platforms, database programming, and finally added some Java and .NET in a wide variety of business domains. He is also a former adjunct professor and a Microsoft Certified Trainer delivering classes on SQL Server and Visual Studio. A full bio can be found at http://www.nokelservices.com/bio.html.

Introduction

Documentation is arguably the least glamorous part of software development. Far from debugging an interesting complex problem or applying a neat new open source library, requirements are often written in terms of customer wants and desires. Technical documentation is closer to writing code, but is still just far enough to be tantalizing.

However, experience bears out that requirements and documentation are key artifacts, especially in large software organizations or organizations where there are many teams participating in the project. Even in an age with a growing use of Agile software development, where there is an emphasis on reduction of rigid formal specifications, there are still many places that will use formal documentation. It may be used exclusively or in some cases in combination with Agile principles. In this book I will discuss formal documentation as a singular process first, then move on to using this documentation in a rigid Waterfall process. Finally I will discuss Agile practices and will demonstrate a way to integrate formal documentation with Agile.

I will define requirements from a couple of different perspectives, discuss how the different perspectives can work together, and list some general recommendations about each. I will also cover the roles the developers play in the requirements process and why developing and interpreting requirements are important skills. Keep in mind that there are many permutations of notations and while many organizations may be similar there may also be slight differences in terminology. For instance, a document that describes the wishes and desires of the business partners could be referred to as a "Business Requirements Definition", "Business Specification", "Requirement Specification", "Business Rules Specification", "Business Function Specification", or similar. No matter the term (or acronym) the end product is a list of features that are desired in the next release of the software.

Likewise, there are many different layouts, formats, templates, and "standard" sections for the actual contents of documentation. This book does not attempt to cover them all, after all it is "Just Enough" to get the reader adept at creating and interpreting requirements, not an exhaustive study of all details in requirements gathering, documentation, or formatting.

Often different requirements are done by different teams. Business requirements may be written by business analysts; functional requirements or logical design may be written by architects. In this book I don't discuss those different roles, only the basics of each type of document. There may be times when developers play the role of business analyst, or architect, and the end product is necessary no matter who writes it.

The Software Development Life Cycle (SDLC) is also a term that can have many meanings, some dated and some brand new. Many people think of the term SDLC as representing a rigid Waterfall development methodology and I will certainly demonstrate it in those terms. However, it can also be applied to Agile because we are still bringing the software "to life" through well-defined principles. This may be a newer (and perhaps controversial) application of SDLC but I will run with it none-the-less.

What this book is about is an introduction to requirements, documentation, and how both formal documentation and informal documentation is used to create working software through various processes. There will be examples that allow the reader to expand their knowledge in whatever environment they are in. Best and/or common practices will be given, with the obvious disclaimer that organizations may have their own process that differ completely in both terms and content. However it is my belief that with the basic knowledge contained in this book most translations of terms and techniques can be done successfully with minimal effort.

Business Requirements

Simply stated, Business Requirements are what the business wants. "Business" in this sense refers to the consumers of the software. Depending on the organization this could be internal business users in other departments, external customers, retail buyers, or the components of a product vision laid out by a marketing team or product lead.

Often a Business Analyst will either produce the Business Requirements Document (BRD) or assist in translating between business customers and technology. Depending on the nature of the software and the stage of the project, they may start with a Primary Business Goal, sometimes referred to as the Vision Statement. This is especially important for brand new software, but can also serve as an import guiding statement when an existing piece of software is undergoing a major enhancement.

A vision statement is just as it sounds – high level and should summarize of overall direction, purpose, or aim for the software being developed. In this book the imaginary software project will be on a donor relations program, the vision for which is shown below.

> To provide managers of non-profit organizations
> the ability to enter and track donations of money
> and time, send follow-ups (both solicitations and
> thank-you notes), and manage contacts and events
> related to donors and volunteers.

Although simple, this statement sums up the high-level purpose of the software. At any point in the discussion of requirements the team can look at the vision statement and see if the requirement being discussed supports the vision statement. If not, the pending requirement may be completely rejected, or maybe included in the requirements but with a low priority or on a "nice to have" list. Perhaps the requirement is valid but is better aligned with a group of requirements for a release further down the road. The vision statement gives the team a litmus test for ultimate authority on requirements and design.

An important item to note is that the vision (and most statements in the next few sections) are written in plain business language, not in technical terms. This is appropriate as statements and documents at this level are intended to be understood and ultimately approved by the business. Technical jargon at this level is easily misunderstood and makes no sense to many consumers of the software. Unless of course you are writing software for technical people!

Another high-level abstraction that is sometime used is a "Use Case Diagram." This is a picture, often associated with Unified Modeling Language (UML). It generally depicts the system as a black box and "actors" as stick figures that interact with various components of the system. While appearing simple Use Case Diagrams are actually very powerful for identifying common user groups, common sub-components of the system, and even interactions between components that may not be obvious when simply listing out actions in a linear fashion.

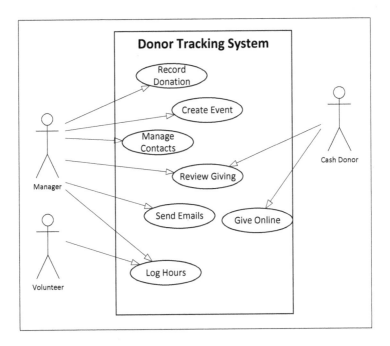

Figure 1 - Use Case Diagram

In the above diagram it can be seen that there are three actors and seven use cases. While many of the use cases apply to only a single actors, it can also be seen that some use cases can be shared among actors. This could imply a need for security or role-based functionality discrimination. The diagram doesn't show any of these restrictions for special conditions. When more detail is needed a diagram can be supplemented by a written use case which can be much more detailed and descriptive.

The format of the written description can vary widely between organizations. And details may also vary based on the complexity of the use case. The example written use case given next includes fields for formal name, author, date, list of actors, description, and more.

Use Case Name:	Log Hours
Created by:	EC
Date Created:	1-6-2017
Actors:	Volunteer, Manager
Description:	Actors should be able to log hours for a given event.
Priority:	1
Assumptions:	Actors set up with proper events. Manager has set up event with proper number of volunteers and timespan.
Rules:	Users must choose a valid event before logging hours. Volunteers can only log hours for themselves. Managers can log hours for themselves as well as enter 'Total Time' for an event. Total time for an event cannot exceed time multiplied by the number of users.
Preconditions:	Actors successfully sign onto the system.
Notes:	

Figure 2 - Written User Case Description

In addition to, or sometimes in place of use case diagrams and descriptions, the BRD may contain a list of requirements in sentence form. Again, the content and format varies widely but the below table is one possible example. Notice that each requirement is given an identifier along with a priority.

ID:	Description	Priority
R-30	Users cannot sign into the system until after they are registered.	Med
R-31	To log hours the user should pick an event first before entering hours.	High
R-32	Managers should be able to create an event with details of time, place, description, and organization.	High
R-33	Managers should be able to enter contacts into the system.	Med
R-34	Managers should be able to record cash donations from donors.	High
R-35	Donors should be able to review their giving statements by year.	High

Figure 3 – Detailed Requirements Table

Note that the sample in Figure 3 is an overly simple example and most likely a real BRD would have additional columns of information. These might be a requirement category, such as "System", "Legal", "Performance", etc. There could also be a "Notes" column for additional information and a "Date" for when the requirement was added. If the project is being done is phases a desired release number could be added. A column for "User Role" could identify which roles, if known, would be players in each of the requirements. Finally, a "How to Test" column is commonly present; this gives the testing team an idea on how to validate the requirement. The main point is that the above statements are from the business perspective and while not technical, care must be taken to understand exactly how a business expectation translates into a technical implementation. It would be either the business analyst's job or a reviewer from the technical team to push back on requirements such as "The System will monitor in real-time all users throughout the world for improper email usage."

One other artifact that may have an alternative representation to the use-case diagram representation of the actors. These are generally summarized as roles although in some cases the individual users who are part of those roles can also be identified. Figure 4 shows an example of a role summary table. If the project is new from scratch this table is important in defining the initial user set. If the project is an enhancement to existing software this table may contain only new or changed roles. Although not shown this table could also be cross-referenced in the detailed requirements table as a column included per requirement.

Role Name:	Description	Users
Manager	Creates events; records donations and volunteer hours; composes and send emails; runs volunteer and donor summary reports.	Tom, Ron, Amy
Volunteer	Registers for events; records service hours.	Added at runtime.
Donor	Donates online; reviews donor summary statements.	Added at runtime.
Administrator	Creates users, maintains type tables, and creates reports.	Ed, Jim
Finance User	Runs donation summary reports and volunteer hour reports.	Andy, Nancy

Figure 4 - Role Summary Table

This table may also identify the existence or need for non-human accounts or roles. These may exist for the system to communicate with a database, web service, or cloud account on behalf of the application and not a particular user or role. If additional logins or accounts are needed directly on other systems they could also be listed here.

Project Requirements

While the previous paragraphs have discussed the actual requirements of the software, the BRD may have many other important project-related sections as well. In general these address aspects of the process or the project and are as much for the project manager as for members of the business or technical teams. They may also be required as part of an auditing or regulatory oversight process. The vision statement was a project-level statement, and there are often others which will be discussed next. Again, there are numerous versions of content and format but several common sections will be demonstrated in the next few pages.

The BRD may contain a list of dependences for the project. Depending on the size and structure of the organization this could be almost anything. One example would be a development project being dependent on a database farm being completed in time. Or developers obtaining licenses for a required piece of software. Or possibly even getting enough development staff. Although in general the list could be quite large it is often sufficient to put the top few dependencies in this area based on a chosen criteria such as risk, probability, cost, or some other criteria.

A list of assumptions is often in the BRD, some of which could tie in quite tightly to the list of dependencies. For example, one assumption could be "Licenses are purchased for all the development team" which may be tied in to a matching dependency.

Others might describe situations that aren't in place when the document was prepared but are expected to be resolved by the time the development is complete. These would be things such as "Quality Assurance Team will be staffed to handle our testing" or "Web servers will be patched to latest version before going to production."

Constraints is also a very common and very important section. This could list pre-conditions that must be met such as "Web Servers must be a patch level 17-02 prior to deployment" or "Database driver version must be 9.10 or greater" to scheduling issues similar to "End of Year Freeze will not be lifted until Feb 1st." While some of the items listed in this section may seem obvious, having them formally stated and part of the project definition leaves little room for ambiguity. Remember that "obvious" is actually a relative term; what is obvious to a business user may not be obvious to a software engineer and vice versa. Whether dealing with inter-departmental customers or external retail users, defining limits for the software sets proper expectations.

Projects may also have a reference section citing other projects or external sources of information. Extending the example above, a reference to the organization freeze calendar may be included. If the project depends on other projects such as a database migration that may be referenced.

Retail software that is to align with a marketing campaign may have a reference to important dates or a copy of the marketing plan attached. Important waivers or certifications can also be attached; copies of service agreements from third-party vendors or internal support teams could go here as well.

Many BRDs are actually "living" documents, meaning they can be changed during the life of the project through proper channels (discussed later in this book). Often the "original" requirement listing is left intact for a proper historical perspective. Any new, changed, or cancelled requirements would generally be listed in a separate section. This would include not only the new requirement and all documentation for it, but a reference to the old requirement if the new one modifies a previously-approved requirement. Additionally, if a BRD is to describe software to be released over multiple cycles a section can describe "future" requirements that would be addressed in subsequent release cycles.

Sometimes the BRD will address a strategy for testing. Testing may be the responsibility of a dedicated Quality Assurance/Testing (QA) team, or testing may be done with a subset of end users. The Testing Strategy section can define how the testing will be done, who will be doing testing, and what is acceptable for the software to be considered passing. This section may also describe the resolution process so that the business, QA, and the development teams are all aware of the process to be followed.

Regulatory requirements may specify that certain projects contain a statement of how the software can be recovered in an emergency. Usually the full Disaster Recovery plan is a completely separate and distinct artifact but a summary can be included in the BRD for completeness. Additionally a link or reference can be included for the complete document. For retail software this could be a description of a stand-alone "live backup and recovery" system.

A Glossary of Terms is often present; this allows for communication roadblocks between business teams and software development teams to be minimized. Reviewers and approvers may not be as familiar with the technical terms or business jargon as the actual authors of the document. Anytime notational short-cuts or acronyms are used in the bulk of the document they should be placed in this section.

In many cases in a formal project the requirements document must be reviewed and approved. This could be mandated by organization policy, regulation, or both. Representatives from both the business (consumer) side and the technical/implementer side may need to approve to signify each understands what the expectations are of what will be delivered. This is often referred to as "sign-off" and in more formal methodologies this is the final stage of requirements before moving on to design.

This area may be broken down into separate sections if some parties need to be reviewers but not necessarily approvers. For example, if the software pulls data from or sends data to other systems, representatives from those systems often would review as well but may or may not need to provide approval depending on the complexity of the interaction. A Marketing team may need to review the document to ensure their marketing plan properly reflects what the software will do.

Functional Design

Another common piece of documentation is the Functional Design Document (FDD), which may be called Functional System Design, Technical Design, or Technical System Design. While the BRD is business oriented with technology as a secondary audience, the FDD is just the opposite. This document generally describes in more technical detail the changes to the current system or design of a new system. The FDD may have many sections in common with the BRD, such as approvals, glossary, reference, or dependencies. When an FDD section does have a common section with the BRD, the FDD's section is usually more technical in nature. Also, in some cases there may be an FSD (Functional System Design) that is architecture-oriented and a Technical System Design (TSD) that is code-oriented. In the following paragraphs I am assuming a single document approach but this can easily be expanded to multiple documents if needed.

The FDD will have functional statements listed in a similar manner to the requirements of the BRD. One important reason to list the functional statements is to make sure that all of the requirements listed in the BRD are addressed. Some FDDs will include a Traceability Matrix that will use the BRD IDs and the FDD IDs to ensure each requirement is covered by a functional statement. Other formats might include the requirement ID directly in the table. The table in Figure 5 included the BRD IDs as one column. Other columns could be included, such as component (GUI, Database, security, etc.)

ID:	Description	BRD-ID
F-10	The system will use an internal database table to track and authenticate users.	R-30
F-11	Events will listed in a dropdown select box; the data coming from a table of Events.	R-31
F-12	The hours input will be disabled until a valid project is chosen.	R-31
F-13	A Manager menu system will be available only to members in the Manager Role.	R-33, R-34
F-14	Contacts, Emails, and Donations will be available on the Managers menu.	R-33, R-34

Figure 5 - Functional Design Statements

If a true matrix is used, it could be as simple as the one shown below.

BRD ID:	BRD Description	Functional ID
R-30	Users should not have to sign into the system; their current network login should be used for identification.	F-10
R-31	To log hours the user should pick an event first before entering hours.	F-11, F-12

Figure 6 - Traceability Matrix

Notice the relational items in Figures 6 and 7 aren't one-to-one; multiple functional statements can cover the same requirement, and multiple requirements may be related to a single functional statement. These cross references are important in that they provide an important check that the design of the system properly implements all the business requirements detailed in the BRD.

The FDD may also go deeper into examining and/or designing infrastructure. A new system would list infrastructure requirements to support the system. These could include web servers, database servers, network support, security and firewall rules, and messaging support if needed. An existing system could list changes or anticipated impact to the current state. The previous statements assume an inter-departmental application inside of an enterprise organization. For a retail application this could be required system support or minimum required hardware.

Technical Design

The FDD often specifies the technical design of the application. Information in this area can include:

- High-level architecture diagram
- Database design diagram
- UML diagrams
- API documentation.

The following paragraphs will discuss each of these and provide examples continuing with the donor manager program we've been working with so far.

A very basic architecture diagram is shown below. Although it appears ubiquitous and non-informative, there are a few important things that can be determined from it. First there is an expectation for both a full-size GUI and a smart phone GUI. Second, there are separate web and database servers. And finally, there are no interactions with other systems.

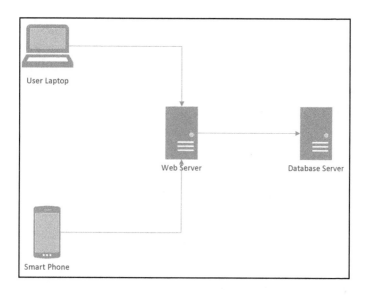

Figure 7 - Basic Architecture Diagram

A more complex diagram is shown in Figure 8; this would be more typical for an internal application in an organization.

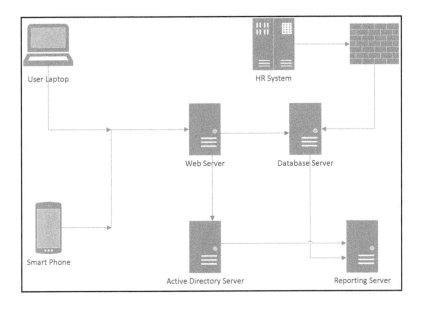

Figure 8 - Advanced Architecture Diagram

In the above diagram there are many interfaces and the system is understandably more complex. There would be logins between systems, schedules, and agreed-upon data formats. Since many more systems are involved there would necessarily be many more reviewers and approvers as discussed in a previous section.

Data modeling and database design is the topic of another "Just Enough" book, but a simplified database diagram will is shown In Figure 9. This is a basic Entity Relationship (ER) diagram for part of the donor application. Four tables are shown – Event_Users, Event, System_User, and Donation. Each table has attributes with associated data types.

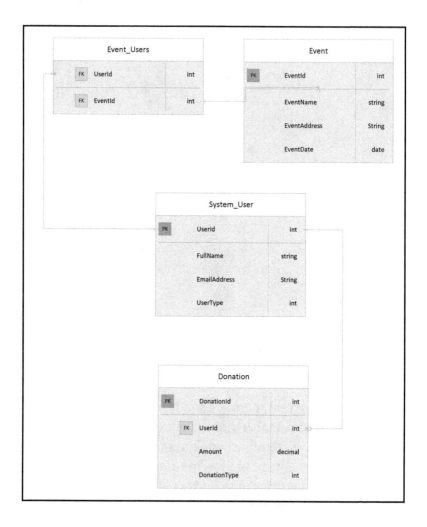

Figure 9 - Simplified Database Diagram

Each table also has a "PK" or "FK" notations, or both. These represent the "primary key" and "foreign key" respectfully.

The primary key is a value that uniquely identifies each row in a table. In many cases this is a value that is generated by the database and is simply an incrementing integer; it is the responsibility of the database software to enforce the uniqueness.

A foreign key is a value in one table that must exist in another table to relate the two tables. In Figure 9, the Donation table is linked to the User table via the UserId column; each value for UserId in Donation must also exist in System_User. This links each donation to a specific user.

More database theory is discussed in another "Just Enough" book dealing with database design and querying.

When applications interface with other systems often there is a data mapping table, sometimes called a data dictionary. This is a listing of data as it moves into or out of the system and can be critical for ensuring compatibility. If fields need transformation between systems this artifact would note that and provide a definition for the transform. If there are many such interfaces or transfers then it is generally clearer to have a separate table for each interaction.

The example in Figure 10 is a sample based on the Donor application. In the architecture diagram in Figure 8 there is an interface between the application and the HR system. For the purpose of demonstration it will be assumed that the Donor program keeps track of volunteer hours and donations within an organization; those users are fed on a weekly basis into the application's database table.

Data Mapping Between HR Database and Donar Database

Source (Table : Column)	Transform	Destination (Table : Column)
User : Firstname, User : Lastname	Firstname + ' ' + Lastname	System_User : FullName
User : Email	None	System_User : EmailAddress
User : u_type_nbr	None	System_User : UserType

Figure 10 - Simple Data Mapping Table

While this is obviously a highly simplified listing there are some very important observations that can be made. First, multiple columns in the source can be combined into a single column in the destination. In the HR database the User table has a column for Firstname and a column for Lastname. These are combined into the System_User:FullName column by a transform that makes a new string.

The reverse is also true. If a source column contains multiple pieces of information that will be mapped to different columns in the destination this could also done via string parsing, splitting, or some other lookup algorithm.
In the example above the situation could just as easily been reversed – HR having a Fullname column and System_User could be defined with separate columns for FirstName and LastName. The lines in the mapping document would then have a slightly more complex transform as shown in Figure 11.

Source (Table : Column)	Transform	Destination (Table : Column)
User : Fullname	Split(' ')[0]	System_User : FirstName
User : FullName	Split(' ')[1]	System_User : LastName

Figure 11 – Multiple Destinations from One Source

The transform could either be real code, pseudo-code, or a long form description. In Figure 11 it is pseudo-code for using a string function to split the entry into an array based on an assumed space between the parts of the name. The first array element is the first name, the second array element is the last name. No error handling is shown. The long form description could take the form of "Split the Fullname into parts and use the first value". This would allow the implementation to choose the proper parsing algorithm, account for errors, three-part names, etc.

Some columns may come in verbatim as shown for the Email column in Figure 10. Although the transform column shows "None" there could alternatively be a validation function there. A regular expression could validate the incoming email was in acceptable format. Or if the column needed a simple format change this could thought of as verbatim but with a minor format change. For example if there was a phone number column it could either be validated or have a simple format change applied. An incoming number of 123.4456.7789 could be changed to (123)4456-7789.

Finally, when a column in the source system has a very cryptic or non-intuitive name the mapping document is invaluable for reference later on. The source column "u_type_nbr" is mapped to the "UserType" column in the destination database. Although there could be some inference there this isn't guaranteed and having an explicit transform defined is a much more sustainable approach.

A class diagram is a representation of the classes that will be coded in the application. Most often this is a UML (Unified Modeling Language) diagram that follows a standard convention and notation. The diagram is often a logical diagram and may or may not be targeted at a certain language. Even when the development language is known the diagram itself is neutral. This allows analysis tools to be used that take the diagram and generate classes in different languages to be used if needed.

Figure 12 shows the beginnings of a class diagram for the Donor application. Although simple (due to space concerns) there are still many concepts that can explained and scaled out if and when needed.

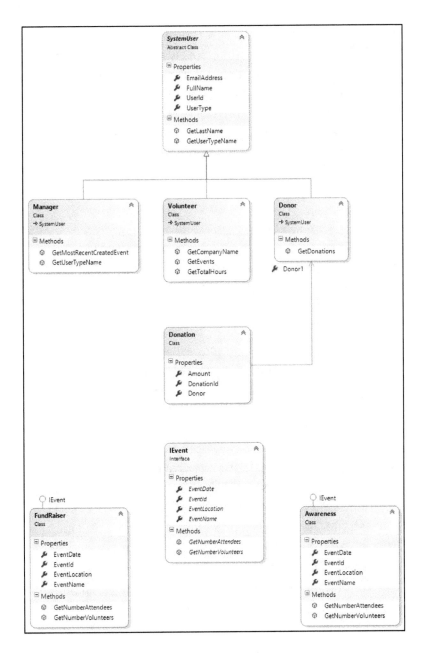

Figure 12 - Class Diagram

The classes in Figure 12 largely represent the tables defined in the database. Objects that closely model the database are commonly known as domain objects; the group of these objects is referred to as the domain model. These allow for working with data table constructs in the code/object world. For example an Event class could be created in code, manipulated, and then saved to the database. The members of the class closely aligning with the database table columns eases this process.

Object-oriented design is also modeled. There is a SystemUser abstract base class from which Manager, Donor, and Volunteer derive. This allows for generic algorithms to be used for SystemUsers with types and specific actions to be determined at run-time. Similar modeling is also done with the IEvent class using an interface instead of an abstract base class. The differences between interfaces and abstract base classes will not be detailed here; the focus is on the presence and representation.

There is also a relation shown from Donation to Donor. Many object-relational frameworks allow for navigation between related objects; this is shown in two forms in the diagram. One is a method relation in the Donor class through the GetDonations() method. The other is through a property relation. Donation has a property of Donor which allows the programmer to get "back" to a Donor object from a Donation object. Object/Relational mapping is discussed in more detail in other books in the series.

Notice also there are visual representations of the properties and the methods. What is not seen in this representation is that each method and property can also specify a return type, access level, arguments, or other attributes typically shown in the "Properties" dialog for each item. In Figures 13 and 14 are two classes generated from the diagram in Figure 12. These were generated by Visual Studio ® and are in C-Sharp; the methods have not be implemented yet (they have to be implemented by hand) and have been collapsed to save space.

```csharp
public abstract class SystemUser
{
    public int UserId...

    public int FullName...

    public int EmailAddress...

    public int UserType...

    public String GetLastName()...

    public virtual string GetUserTypeName()...
}
```

Figure 13 - Generated Base Class

```
public class Donor : SystemUser
{
    public List<Donation> GetDonations()...
}
```

Figure 14 - Generated Derived Class

Another type of diagram is the sequence diagram. This diagram shows the flow of an action. This flow can be represented at several levels, from the method call and return value level to an overall object interaction level. Practical examples could include actions such as creating a volunteer event or producing a report. Higher level flows may be logging into the system or sending an email.

Figure 15 shows the sequence diagram for a user reviewing the giving of a donor using a report. From a code perspective a SystemUser object will use a ReportFactory to create an instance of a GivingReport. Then the GenerateReport method will be called, which goes to the DonorDateLayer to get the actual data. Finally the fully created report will be returned to the user.

The vertical squares represent the lifetime of the objects; messages are represented by horizontal lines. It can be seen that the factory is only around long enough to create a report. Also, it only details the interactions between the different objects and the overall flow of the operation, now how the report will be displayed. In this example parameters or conditions aren't noted (i.e. the parameter to the factory signifying a donor report) but some diagrams may show this type of supplemental information.

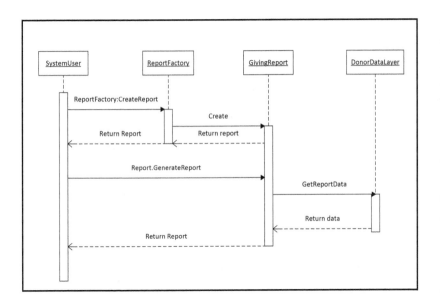

Figure 15 - Giving Report Generation

A sequence diagram at a higher level would appear similar but instead of internal objects or classes external subsystems would be specified. For example, a login flow might have to go from the system out to Active Directory® to get the authentication for a user login request. If that call is successful another system may be contacted to obtain authorization and the role information for a user. This diagram would have those external system names (i.e. Internal Active Directory, Auth Database, etc) in place of the objects represented in Figure 15.

Often times the Functional Design will include mock-ups of the desired screen layout, also known as wire frame diagrams. There are many software packages that handle this sort of "rough sketch" capability, from Excel to Visio. With drag-and-drop design capability, some users may even use the Form Designer in Visual Studio for quick outlines. These can then be translated by the implementation team into whatever display technology the end product will use.

The Wire Frame in Figure 16 represents the desired look for the main page of the Donor application. A standard menu is at the top with a list of events on the left and a tabbed display area on the right. This abstract form could be taken and rendered as a desktop application or a web site. Additional specialty displays, such as small mobile device screens, could also be shown.

Main or alternative displays could be specified in a written description as well. The simple GUI in Figure 16 could also have the following written description:

"The main application screen will have top menu with entries for "Home", "Tools", and "Admin". Below the menu will be the main display area, broken in half horizontally. The left side will contain a list of current and upcoming events. The right side will consist of a tabbed area for displaying "Reminders", "Donors", and "Leads.""

"A small form-factor mobile screen would have the menu as a standard mobile menu and would display the Events Lists as the initial screen. There would be an additional menu item for navigating to the Reminders section, which would then have the other tabs available as part of a swipe control."

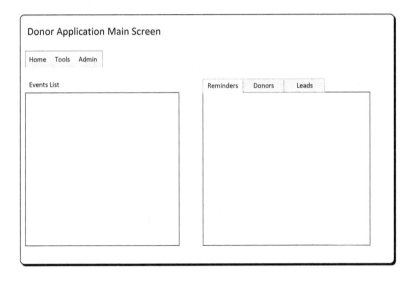

Figure 16 - Simple Wire Frame

Detailed technical documentation can contain function/method specifications as well. This can be done at the external API level (what is exposed to any client programs), the class function level (each class at the domain or business rule layer), or both. It can be documented by hand using a standard format or template and maintaining as necessary. A more common method in recent years has been by generation tools using a standard commenting format in the code, also known as "doc comments." During the compilation process a special flag can be used to generate the documentation so it can be kept up to date with each compile.

Many stand-alone tools are also available that can produce documentation without needing a code compiler. Tools can usually output documentation in multiple formats; from HTML to XML to Helpfile format. The examples below are from Visual Studio in C#.

```
/// <summary>
/// Returns the total dollar value by adding
/// cash donations, in-kind donations, and volunteer
/// hours.
/// </summary>
/// <param name="d">Donor to collect data about.
/// </param>
/// <returns>Dollar amount representing combined
/// value.</returns>
/// <remarks>
/// In-kind donation values are retrieved from the
/// AllowableValues table, are calculated from the
/// EventHoursRate table.
/// </remarks>
public double GetDonorTotalValue(Donor donor)
{ }
```

Figure 17 - .NET Documentation Comments

Notice the formatting that specifies the documentation section is a special form of comment notation – triple slashes instead of the double slash for standard comments. Within these comments pre-defined xml tags are used to delineate sections. The tags shown in Figure 17 are some of the most common tags, there are others for code samples, references, and more. The language/tool documentation would have a more complete listing.

When processed through Visual Studio an xml file is generated that has constituent parts that match the tags in the comments. A portion of the raw output dealing with only the method is shown in Figure 18. The file is much larger than this as each assembly in the project is described in detail, with each method listed and even a basic compiler-generated summary if no user-defined comments are included.

```
<doc>
<assembly>
  <name>DonorAppTC</name>
</assembly>
<members>
  <member name =
"M:DonorAppTC.DonorUtilities.GetDonorTotalValue(Donor
AppTC.Donor)" >
    <summary>
      Returns the total dollar value by adding
      cash donations, in-kind donations, and volunteer
      hours.
    </summary>
    <param name = "donor" >Donor to collect data about.
    </param>
    <returns>Dollar amount representing combined value.
    </returns>
    <remarks>
      In-kind donation values are retrieved from the
      AllowableValues table, volunteer hour values are
      calculated from the EventHoursRate table.
    </remarks>
    </member>
</members>
</doc>
```

Figure 18 - xml Output File

The output from the .NET documentation generator is nothing other than a straight xml file. As stated before, other tools can generate many different output formats; some generating html directly. For the Visual Studio-generated xml file, the raw xml can be processed using any number of methods that can read the xml document and produce an output.

One is XSLT transform language. This is a processing language which renders html and gives the author complete control over how to render the document. The advantage of using this type of processing is that a common format can be designed and then applied to any documentation file produced by the compiler. The xml file could include company header or division information, standard colors, etc. Once the file is defined, a simple reference to it is added to the generated file, then the file can be opened in any web browser.

For example, if the xml stylesheet was called "donor-documentation-processor.xsl" then in each xml documentation file a reference line would be added to reference that file. This is shown in the Figure below.

```
<?xml-stylesheet href="donor-documentation-
processor.xsl" type="text/xsl"?>
<doc>
<assembly>
  <name>DonorAppTC</name>
</assembly>
<!-- previously shown code removed -->
</doc>
```

Figure 19 - Referencing an xsl stylesheet

A portion of the xsl transformation file is shown in Figure 20. Other texts exist for learning XSLT and that will not be discussed in this book. However the sample should give the reader an idea of how XSLT and html can be combined. Normal html tags are used; there are also additional sections for styles that are not shown. This would be key to consistently formatting help files; referencing a standard stylesheet would allow consistency between many different documentation files.

The output is shown in Figure 21. This is a snapshot taken from a browser application. Referring to the code in Figure 20 allows the reader to compare the xsl file to the output. Notice as an example the value of the assembly name. In Figure 19 that value is in the `<name>` tag under `<assembly>`, which is under `<doc>`. In the xsl file this is stored in a local variable, `assemblyName`, which is found with by `select="doc/assembly/name"`. That value is used later as part of the "Assembly Documentation" statement. The output also contains descriptions from the generated `Form1` class which is the application main form. So both custom user documentation and system generated documentation is produced.

The use of xsl processing and the XPath language is out of scope for this discussion; there are many detailed references and tutorials elsewhere and online. Most modern browsers will process xml/xsl files to render a final document, so this approach is a simple and consistent one. However, as mentioned before, there are several other possibilities for rendering the content, the reader is encouraged to explore many others to examine all the possibilities.

```
<?xml version="1.0" encoding="UTF-8" ?>
<xsl:stylesheet version="1.0"
xmlns:xsl="http://www.w3.org/1999/XSL/Transform">
  <!-- Display a documentation file generated by
Visual Studio from XML comments. -->
  <xsl:variable name="assemblyName">
    <xsl:value-of select="doc/assembly/name"/>
  </xsl:variable>
  <xsl:template match="doc">
  <html>
  <head>
    <title>.NET XML Documentation </title>
  </head>
  <body>
    <h2>Documentation Web File</h2>
    <b><u>
      <xsl:value-of select="$assemblyName"/> Assembly
Documentation
    </u></b>
    <p />
    <xsl:apply-templates select="members"/>
  </body>
  </html>
  </xsl:template>

  <!-- Many statements removed for space concerns -->

    <xsl:apply-templates select="summary"/>
    <xsl:apply-templates select="param"/>
    <xsl:apply-templates select="returns"/>
    <xsl:apply-templates select="remarks"/>

    <xsl:template match="summary">
      <i><span class="listItem">- Summary: </span> </i>
      <xsl:value-of select="."/>
      <br />
    </xsl:template>
</xsl:stylesheet>
```

Figure 20 - XSLT Processing Statements

Documentation Web File

DonorAppTC Assembly Documentation

DonorUtilities

`GetDonorTotalValue(DonorAppTC.Donor)`

- *Summary:* Returns the total dollar value by adding cash donations, in-kind donations, and volunteer hours.
- *Param:* **donor:** Donor to collect data about.
- *Returns:* Dollar amount representing combined value.
- *Remarks:* In-kind donation values are retrieved from the AllowableValues table, volunteer hour values are calculated from the EventHoursRate table.

Form1

`components`

- *Summary:* Required designer variable.

Form1

`Dispose(System.Boolean)`

- *Summary:* Clean up any resources being used.
- *Param:* **disposing:** true if managed resources should be disposed; otherwise, false.

Figure 21 - XML file displayed in a browser.

In the earlier section for the BRD it was mentioned that an approver section was generally part of that document. The Functional Design often has a similar section for approvers and reviewers. However, both the BRD and the FSD often are "living" documents, meaning they can change over time.

In many cases changing an approved and reviewed document isn't as simple as merely updating a requirement or changing a class diagram. Often any change to any approved document has to go through a documentation, review, and approval process itself. This is often referred to as the Change Control Process and the actual document is referred to as the Change Request. This process is followed for changes to information already in the document or for adding new information. New information is commonly a new business requirement but could also be new technical or functional information.

There are numerous formats for a Change Request (CR) document. Some are completely generic, meaning they can be used for any change on a project. Others are type-specific and will have different formats for changing the BRD as opposed to changing the FDD or Technical Design. Keep in mind that the location of the change may impact other areas, so a change in a business requirement will most likely also require a change in Functional and/or Technical Design. A change in the Functional or Technical Design typically won't result in a change to Business Requirements but is commonly communicated to the Business because it may have an impact on schedule, resources, etc.

Figure 22 has an example of a CR representing a new business requirement that was left out of the original BRD.

CR-0001

Description: New Requirement for Volunteers to review their total hours served per year.

BRD Information:

BRD-ID	Existing?	Description
R-55	No	Volunteers should to be able to see their total volunteer hours for a given year.

FSD Information:

FSD-ID	Existing?	Description
F-61	No	The Volunteer object will have a method to retrieve total volunteer hours for a given year.

Technical design changes:

The Volunteer class will add an overload of the GetTotalHours method that will take an integer argument specifying the year. This method will have a completely separate query to return the hours for the user in a given year.

New Test Case(s)? Yes.
Describe: Validate user can choose a year to view hours. Compare results with known quantity.

Figure 22 - Sample CR document.

To summarize, the previous sections were all about requirements and documentation. Many simple examples of business requirements, functional design, and technical design and documentation were shown and discussed. Common artifacts such as accountability matrices, UML diagrams, and wire frames were shown. Also, documentation generation through language constructs and XML processing were demonstrated.

Many of the above documents are typically used in formal project management governed projects, usually in a project structure known as waterfall. In the next section of the book, Development Methodologies, the two most prevalent project frameworks will be discussed starting with waterfall. Waterfall breaks down into standard waterfall and iterative waterfall. While these methods are several decades old and stem from more traditional engineering projects, they are still in active use in many organizations due to habit, engrained culture, regulatory oversight, or other factors.

Finally I will discuss one of the fastest growing methodologies for developing software, Agile. Agile is almost the diametric opposite of waterfall and several of its tenants will be discussed and demonstrated. In addition, some common digital agile tools will be shown. The section will end by tying back to formal documentation by discussing a possible method of combining formal documentation with Agile frameworks.

Development Methodologies

Software development organizations often make use of a standard workflow when developing software. This is known in general as the software development process or software development life cycle (SDLC). As noted at the end of the last chapter, the methodology used to implement the life cycle loosely fall into two approaches: traditional project management based processes, such as Waterfall, and less restrictive empirical processes such as Agile. Both development types will be discussed and demonstrated in the following sections.

Waterfall

Waterfall is a sequential process for software development that stems from project methodologies of "classical" engineering such as civil or mechanical. This process usually has several distinct types of activities:

- Requirements
- Design
- Implementation
- Testing
- Integration
- Deployment
- Maintenance

The first part of this book demonstrated typical documentation for the first two items; refer back to that for specific examples.

Below is a general description of each activity and the roll each plays in the overall process.

Activity	Description
Requirements	Gathering and documenting what functionality the users of the system or the product owner want to see as the end product.
Design	Architecting the construction specifics of the system. This could include hardware, the internal functionality and classes, and the specifics of the user interface. Also, specifications on communicating with other systems and the impact
Implementation	The actual building and coding of the system.
Testing	Testing the completed product. This is usually done by a dedicated Quality Assurance (QA) team. The coded system is tested and compared against the requirements for correct functionality.
Integration	Combining the new code with existing code, or a new system within an existing application infrastructure. There is also typically integration testing in this phase.
Deployment	Releasing the new code or system to the general user population.
Maintenance	Ongoing bug fixes and minor enhancements to released software.

Figure 23 - Waterfall Phases of Development

Again, these phases of development are sequential. This means each phase must be complete before the following phase is started. The term "waterfall" comes how this is often graphically represented. Figure 24 shows a common picture interpreted as each block being done before work starts on the next block. Note that the length of each of these is not necessarily uniform. Requirements may take one week while design may take four. Deployment one day.

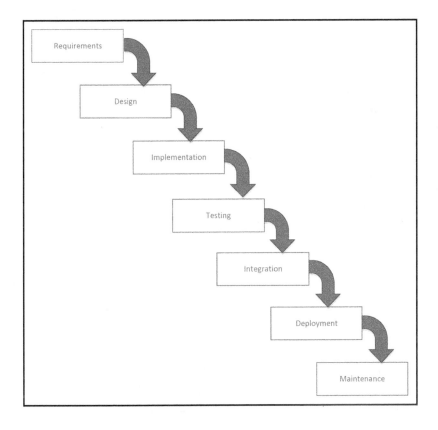

Figure 24 - Waterfall Diagram

Implementation is the actual writing of the code and can use many methodologies. Normally project managers will work with technology teams to develop a Gantt chart or some form of task-based tracking facility to measure the project progress. This has tasks and their estimated lengths and dependencies (if any).

There may even be multiple Gantt charts per project. One for the entire project and one for the development phase is typical. This could be the case if there is more than one project manager on a project. Often there is technology-specific project manager that may have a Gantt chart with much higher detail than the overall project manager for the implementation and test phases.   A simple example is shown below in Figure 25.

ID	Task Name	Start	Finish	Duration
1	Code Data Model	3/6/2017	3/8/2017	3d
2	Unit Tests for Data Model	3/9/2017	3/10/2017	2d
3	Business Layer Coding	3/13/2017	3/22/2017	8d
4	Basic Login	3/9/2017	3/9/2017	1d
5	Admin Display	3/23/2017	3/29/2017	5d

Figure 25 - Simple Gantt Chart

Testing is generally handled by a testing team, commonly referred to as Quality Assurance (QA). These teams use test scripts and/or test plans to ensure the final release software matches what has been defined in the BRD. The tests can either be run by hand or in many cases automated tools exist. Complete coverage of the QA process will not be discussed in this book, but for completeness an example of a manual test script is show in Figure 26.

The testing phase may also include load testing and/or penetration/security testing handled by a special security team. If the application has minimum response time requirements or simultaneous user requirements these will also be tested; this is known as load testing and/or stress testing.

The job of the developer during these testing phases is to respond to the results produced by the testing teams by fixing any bugs found or addressing issues in the security/performance testing.

Test Case Name/ID:	Test Volunteer Log Hours (TC-11)		
BRD-IDs:	R-39, R-40, R-42		
Actor:	Volunteer		
Pre-Conditions:	Tester logged in as Vol_User_1. Valid Events have been populated.		

Steps:

#	Description	Expected Result	P/F
1	User navigates to volunteer event screen	Volunteer events screen display; events shown.	
2	User selects event "Test Event One".	"Test Event One" highlighted, "Enter Hours" button becomes enabled.	
3	User enters 40 hours of service and presses "Save"	Entry is flagged and user sees popup stating "Hours entered cannot be more than event hours"	
4	Users enters 4 hours of service and presses "Save"	Dialog appears stating "Thanks for your service" and goes away after 2 seconds.	
5	User logs out of system; logins again.	User logged back into system.	
6	User navigates to volunteer event screen.	User on volunteer event screen; sees 4 hours for "Test Event One"	

Notes:

Figure 26 - Example Manual Test Case

One can quickly see how this process can often cause issues, particularly with scheduling. For example, what do the developers do while the requirements are being analyzed and documented? How about the testers – their job during development is what? Test cases need developed but that can be done as soon as the BRD is complete. And if a bug is found during testing that necessitates a design or requirements change, how does the time required to complete the Change Request process impact everything else?

Iterative Waterfall

One approach to eliminating the aforementioned scheduling issues in traditional Waterfall is to break the project up in to "phases" so that instead of having one "big bang" software release at the end of the project there are smaller, shorter releases. There are several variations of this, but overall this is classified as Iterative Waterfall. A few of the specific methodologies that formalize the process are knows as Spiral Development, Incremental Development, and Rapid Application Development. Each of these have a set a practices that define the specifics of their methodology. Details of each will not be elaborated on here but I will discuss in general how Iterative Waterfall is accomplished.

In Iterative Waterfall, the overall project may have a detailed BRD, but only part of that BRD will be implemented in each phase. Each phase will have a complete set of documentation and follow the waterfall flow. The approval process for each document/stage is still enforced. Once a document is approved any change must still follow the change control process. With phases the idea is that each work group can be on a different phase in such a way that the idle time can be minimized. Only phase one will have the full effect of the idle-time issue; after that the analysts and designers work one phase ahead of the developers and testers so that as one develop/test phase is completed the next phase has been designed and is ready to be coded. This method of overlapping phases allows for teams to remain busy throughout the lifecycle of the project.

There are two ways to schedule releases of software when using an iterative process. One is to specify a releasable feature set and based on the overall plan and in which phase that will be complete, set the release date at the end of that phase. This is often done with retail software as the next feature set is defined as the next major version. The outside appearance of the major version release masks the fact that the product was developed with an incremental process.

The other way to schedule releases is to make a standardized release schedule and release completed software on that date. Depending on the length of the phases an organization might have a release at the end of each quarter, or two or three times a year. In this manner the feature set continually grows. Sometimes this is combined with major features in that the quarterly releases are considered "patches" in between the major releases.

Waterfall development, whether iterative or traditional, is typically documentation heavy. The next section discusses almost the polar opposite – lightweight agile development.

Agile Development

While waterfall methodologies attempt to define a repeatable process for constructing software, agile methodologies take a radically different approach. Agile methodologies acknowledge change and actually embrace it as part of the process. The complete history and discussion of the Agile Manifesto for software development will not be fully discussed here; many excellent resources are available for that. However, from the agile manifesto site (http://http://agilemanifesto.org/) here are the principles of agile:

Individuals and interactions over processes and tools
Working software over comprehensive documentation
Customer collaboration over contract negotiation
Responding to change over following a plan

That is, while there is value in the items on
the right, we value the items on the left more.

Figure 27 - Principles of the Agile Manifesto

Rather than a strictly defined rigid and repeatable process, Agile development is an example of empirical process control (Schwaber 2004). The workflow is designed for rapid response to change with the intended result of lessoning the impact of customers changing their mind. The next several sections will explain and demonstrate the most common agile development frameworks – Scrum, XP, and Kanban.

Scrum

Scrum is a framework that was developed in the 1990s. It is a "framework" in that it suggests a standard set of practices around managing a project but doesn't specify the details of the actual implementation. The main ideas of Scrum are:

- Time-boxed meetings and events.
- Short iteration cycles.
- Small self-organizing teams.
- Transparency of all project artifacts.

The central concept in Scrum that transcends all other categories is the Sprint. This is the time-boxed development cycle in which most things happen. The Scrum Guide (Schwaber and Sutherland 2016) calls for the Sprint to be thirty calendar days or less. In practice it is commonly two or three weeks – ten to fifteen working days. It is iterative and should be the same length for the duration of the project.

By the end of each Sprint a piece (or pieces) of potentially shippable software is able to be produced. The Product Owner (described later) decides whether or not to release/ship the newly coded software. Normally a formal release consists of many Sprints that incrementally build releasable pieces.

To formally define the remaining aspects of the Scrum framework there are three categories of definitions: the artifacts, the team, and the meetings. Each of these will be defined and some practical examples will be shown. Many of the following descriptions can be referenced in the Scrum Guide (Schwaber and Sutherland 2016).

Unlike all the documentation described in the first part of this book, Scrum has very few and somewhat simplistic artifacts. And since Scrum is a framework the actual format of these artifacts is not prescribed in detail, only that they exist. Teams are able to use a format that is familiar and easy to understand for them.

Scrum artifacts consist of:

- Product Backlog
- Sprint Backlog
- Working software.

From the specification of the framework, that's it. However there are several additional artifacts that are considered common extensions that I will discuss as well:

- Burndown/Burnup chart
- Impediment List

The Product Backlog is a priority-ordered list of desired functionality in the application. This is often thought of as a list of requirements but they are typically in a different form and at a higher level of abstraction. These stories are written in plain business language. Although there are many formats, the simple way to express a backlog item is as a 'user story' with the general form of "As a <user role> I would like to <do something> so that <business value>." These can represent either large or small pieces of work; stories small enough to include in a sprint or larger stories known as "Epics". Epics are generally broken into Sprint-sized stories before being worked on.

Some example Product Backlog/User Stories are shown in Figure 28.

As a Manager I need to create an event so that volunteers can register for working the event.

As a Volunteer I need to log my hours at an event so that both myself and the event owner can track my volunteer hours.

As a Manager I need to review the volunteer hours for each event so I can know which events are overstaffed.

As a Manager I need to review cash giving so I can send thank you notes.

Figure 28 - User Stories in the Product Backlog

While the Product Owner is responsible for ordering the backlog by priority, the Development Team is responsible for estimating the level of effort for each story. This estimate is only a relative effort, often done with abstract values that only show relation to each other and not total effort. There are many different schemes that teams can use such as "T-Shirt sizes (small/medium/large) or a Fibonacci value system. This is done using a small reference story as a "1" and ranking all other stories relatively. A "2" is roughly twice as much effort, a "5" is five times the effort.

Whichever way is used the Development Team, over a period of Sprints, will become comfortable with the number of stories that can be done in a single Sprint. Five smalls and two mediums, one large and three mediums, 22 points, 35 points, etc. Then based on the story estimates and the "velocity" the Development Team decides how many stories they can accomplish in the next Sprint. These stories then become part of the Sprint Backlog.

The Sprint Backlog is entirely the responsibility of the Development Team. It contains each of the Product Backlog items and the plan for implementing each one. The plan is represented as tasks and represents the actual work items that the team must do to complete each story. These tasks are usually thought of as half a day or less; this is the first time that hours are considered in the process. An example of Sprint backlog items is in Figure 29.

The Sprint Backlog is always open and visible, but only the Development Team manages it. From a practical perspective both the Product Backlog and Sprint Backlog items are usually written on small individual note cards. This allows for easily shuffling and rearranging as well as preventing too much detail for stories or tasks. Ideally both backlogs are available and visible to all parties at all times.

As a Manager I need to review cash giving so I can send thank you notes. (Small)	
	Add menu item only for Managers role. (0.5d)
	Implement initial GUI screen with search criteria. (3 d)
	DAO Objects and query for returning search results. (2d)
	Display grid for results. (1d)

Figure 29 - Sprint Backlog Example

Notice is this example the story is sized as "Small" and each of the tasks are given a time estimate. These will be used later when I discuss monitoring progress.

As noted above at the end of each sprint the Development Team demonstrates the working software. This is potentially shippable software meaning that no more work is needed on this item before it is released to the end user. This is the "ultimate" artifact of any software project – working software.

This can sometimes be confusing and a common question is this – "Does working software get released at the end of each sprint?" The answer is "it depends", as when to release completed software is solely the decision of the Product Owner. The key is that the working software is "potentially" shippable.

For example a Product Backlog item may address the need for a menu system. The menu system can be complete even if the "targets" of each item do not exist. The menu itself would require no more work before the official release but the targets of each menu item would be developed in a subsequent sprint. In this case the menu is "potentially" shippable but doing so would probably not be chosen.

The following sections discuss the non-specified but often-used additional artifacts. These add to the transparency of the system and can generally promote better efficiency. Again there is no iron-clad definition of content so different teams may have different representations of the data each artifact contains.

The Sprint Backlog is often displayed on a Sprint Task Board, with columns for work "to-do", "in-progress", and "done." This board is updated often, at least once a day, and is a visual representation of the team's progress through the work items. For "analog" boards stories and tasks are written on notes or index cards and can be easily moved as needed. Digital boards will be covered later in the book.

The board also contains a burndown chart which is a measure of how much work is remaining in a sprint. Ideally this would be smooth graph from "all work remaining" at the beginning of the first day to "all work complete" at the end of the last day. Depending on how the team represents their sprint backlog items the chart can have different axes. The time axis is generally days in the sprint, but the vertical axis can be story points, tasks, task-days, or whatever makes sense for the team.

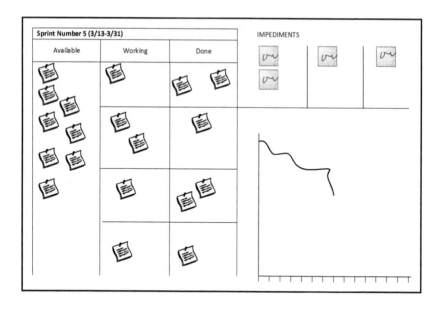

Figure 30 - Sample Sprint Task Board

A sample task board is shown in Figure 30. The horizontal breaks in the working and done columns provide an area for each developer. Again, keeping with transparency it is easy for the entire team to see what has been done, what is left to do, and who is working on each task.

Notice there is also a section titled "Impediments." These are items that are preventing the Development Team from completing a task or a problem they would like solved to improve the process. This can be a technical issue such as "lack of dedicated test environment" or an environmental or team issue such as "Waiting on clarification for story 2."

There are only three defined roles in the Scrum team – the Product Owner, the Scrum Master, and the Development Team. In total a team is generally suggested to be less than eight people, but again, this is only a suggestion. Teams are to be self-organizing so larger teams could potentially have problems of organization.

The Product Owner is the individual responsible for prioritizing features to be developed and evaluating those features after development. In even simpler terms the product owner represents the customers and/or stakeholders and ensures the development effort satisfies their desires. They possess the vision for the product but do not have the means to write it.

The Product Owner fulfills their duty by managing the Product Backlog and being available to the development team. This provides for development to be done in the proper order with the most important items done first. Being available to the development team enables timely clarification of functionality questions and allows for quicker overall development.

The Scrum Master is mainly responsible for explaining and enforcing the rules of Scrum, both to the rest of the team as well as to those outside of the team. This involves facilitating meetings as well as coaching the other members of the team, product planning, and ensuring the end product's value is maximized. Also, understanding any procedures which could be hindering the team or organization from implementing an effective Scrum process.

Items that are restricting the process are often referred to as "impediments"; these were first shown in Figure 30. Having the Scrum Master work on these frees the developers to fulfill their main purpose – developing.

Often times those familiar with waterfall will want to ascribe the same duties as a typical Project Manager has, but the Scrum Master role is different. Rather than being a 'director' assigning tasks and monitoring progress, the Scrum Master is a facilitator and encourager to the rest of the team. While the development team is in their development cycle the Scrum Master's main job is to run the daily meetings and assist the team to remove road blocks or impediments.

The Development Team is comprised of the individuals that actually produce the working code. This is a truly cross-functional team and Scrum disallows titles other than "Team Member". Even if the organization has developers, testers, and database administrators in Scrum they are simply team members.

The team is self-organizing and self-accountable. No one tells the team what or how to do any task items, but there is also no single point of failure or scapegoat; the team succeeds or fails as a whole. This team arrangement allows for maximum flexibility and theoretically an increase in productivity. Anyone can work on what needs done next if they possess the appropriate knowledge, or can learn the skills during the sprint. Rather than working for someone not in the team such as a traditional project manager, the teams helps and mentors one another if needed to ensure the entire sprint effort succeeds.

As mentioned earlier, the team is also responsible for estimating the stories. Two methods – t-shirt and Fibonacci were mentioned. The team chooses one of these (or something else entirely) and defines how they are used.

If the team chooses t-shirt sizing, they pick what defines each size. "Small" could be less than a day, "medium" between a day and one week, "large" is over one week of effort. Keeping track of how many of each they team can accomplish in a Sprint allows them to consistently choose the correct number and mixture of stories.

Using Fibonacci numbers is often referred to as "story points" because each story will get a number. These numbers are not linear; each number represents the sum of the previous two numbers: 0, ½, 1, 2, 3, 5, 8, 13, 21, 34, 55, 89, and 144. A small reference story is chosen and assigned the value of "one". Then each story is compared to the reference story and assigned a value in terms of multiples of effort.

The developers should agree on the final estimate. If an agreement can't be reached a game called "Planning Poker" is often played. This game uses a special deck (or app) that has the numbers (or sometimes a modified Fibonacci sequence) on each card. The developers discuss a story, then each player displays a card with their estimate. If the numbers are wildly different (say 3, 13, and 34) the reasoning behind each person's estimate is discussed. Then the team will vote again. This will continue until a defined stopping point is reached; either a specified number of voting rounds or until the numbers are within a certain range such as three consecutive numbers.

The final number can be an average. The story is then referred to as "three point" story. The total number of points for the completed stories each Sprint would be the team's velocity.

There are four prescribed meetings in Scrum. Each is time-boxed, meaning that it has a fixed duration and cannot go longer than the prescribed time. It is the Scrum Master's job to enforce these limits.

The Sprint Planning Meeting is where the work for the upcoming Sprint is planned. The entire team – Scrum Master, Product Owner, and Development Team participate in this meeting. Depending on how teams arrange their Sprints this meeting either occurs right before the Sprint starts or on day one of the sprint. This meeting is time-boxed to eight hours for a 30 day sprint. This generally scales pretty well; 30 calendar days is approximately 22 working days; so for a two week sprint (10 working days) a four hour meeting is generally adequate.

The meeting is broken into two parts. The first part, one quarter of the time, is for the Product Owner and the Development Team to decide which items from the Product Backlog will be done in the Sprint. The Product Owner should have prioritized the backlog before the meeting, so based on the Team's known (or estimated) velocity and their estimates of the backlog stories they can determine how many to attempt. In addition, the entire Scrum team should agree on a Sprint Goal that summarizes the focus of this Sprint. This could a be statement about a common component or subsystem being developed or more general statement such as "Improve the user experience".

The Product Owner has the final say on which stories they want, but the development team has the final say on the number of stories included. In this way a conversation can be had regarding choosing which stories make it. If the top five stories in absolute priority are too big, the Product Owner may choose the top four plus a smaller less important story. Or after discussing one of the stories further the team decides that what they initially estimated as a large story is actually a smaller story. This process highlights the importance of face-to-face interaction and active discussion leading to maximizing product value.

The second part of the meeting is for the Development Team to break the stories into tasks or work items, thus generating the details of the Sprint Backlog. The Scrum Master and the Product Owner are still present, but only for answering questions and clarifications. Tasks and their estimates are the product of and owned by the team. At the end of the meeting there should be enough clearly stated tasks to start the sprint. The Development Team should have a clear idea of the tasks ahead, and the Product Owner should know what will be delivered at the end of the Sprint.

Once the Sprint begins, the Scrum Master facilitates a meeting known as the Daily Scrum. This meeting should be held at the same time every day and is time-boxed to 15 minutes. It is for the Development Team to do a quick review of the previous day's development, state their plans for the next day, and state any impediments to progress. Generally this is done by each developer, one-at-a-time, briefly answering three questions:

- What was done yesterday?
- What will be done today?
- Are there any impediments blocking the work?

The Sprint Task Board is updated during this meeting. At the conclusion of the meeting the developers and the Scrum Master have tasks for the upcoming day. If there are any questions about statements made during the meeting, those are addressed in separate meetings, either impromptu person-to-person discussions or scheduled formal meetings. However it is the intention that daily short meetings and impromptu discussions, along with the actions of the Scrum Master to work on impediments, will lessen the need for formal scheduled meetings.

At the end of each Sprint the Sprint Review meeting is held. This is also time-boxed; four hours for a 30-day sprint or linearly scaled down as noted before. The Scrum Master, Development Team, and Product Owner all attend, as well as any customers/stakeholders invited by the Product Owner.

Several things happen during the Sprint Review. If the Product Owner invited stakeholders he/she will explain to them the backlog items that were selected and completed during the Sprint. The Development Team will demonstrate the completed items and discuss any questions with the Product Owner and stakeholders. The Scrum Master and Development Team may discuss what impediments they overcame. The Product Owner may discuss the next set of items in the Product Backlog or the Backlog as a whole to see if priorities have changed.

The result of the Sprint Review is that the Product Owner (and stakeholders) see the Development Team making progress. Frequent review and feedback also allow for quickly changing direction should outside forces affect the project. Coming out of the Sprint Review the Product Backlog should be well-organized to go into the next Sprint Planning meeting.

Another meeting held at the end of each Sprint is the Sprint Retrospective. It is also time-boxed to three hours for a 30-day Sprint and scaled as appropriate. This is also for the entire Scrum Team but no stakeholders should attend.

During this meeting the team reviews its own process during the last Sprint. Any areas that were problematic can be identified so the team can work to improve them and thereby improve their efficiency. The Scrum Master may also present resolved impediments here as well as take any identified items as new impediments. The focus of this meeting is for the team to improve themselves.

Although those are the only meetings prescribed in the Scrum Guide (Schwaber and Sutherland 2016) there is one other meeting that is commonly held during the Sprint. Since it isn't defined in the Guide it may be called different names such as "Backlog Grooming" or "Product Backlog Refactoring". Whatever the name the intent is the same – to have a formal meeting once or twice during the Sprint to work on the Product Backlog. While no time-box value is specified it is generally preferred to keep this meeting to an hour or less since it occurs during the Sprint and any longer may disrupt the team's work.

The advantage to do having this meeting during the Sprint is that it can often make the subsequent Sprint Planning meeting shorter. Developers may have found something while coding current task items that affect backlog item size estimates and communicating that immediately to the Product Owner could alter priorities. Or the Product Owner might need to rearrange items due to changing business conditions. Whatever the cause, communicating these things and constantly updating the Product Backlog can make the entire process more efficient.

Over the years a term that has grown in popularity and aptly describes the struggle Scrum has encountered, especially in large organizations where traditional project management techniques are entrenched. That term is "ScurmButt" and arises from the phrase "We do Scrum, but..." followed by some sort of deviation from the prescribed Scrum framework. I will not discuss the details here, just note that it exists.

Extreme Programming (XP)

Extreme Programming is another Agile development methodology. It is more prescriptive than Scrum in that it specifies specific coding techniques to use as part of the process. While some aspects are shared, such as short development cycles, a sustainable pace, and collective code ownership/shared responsibility are similar to Scrum there are a few additional specifications that make XP unique. In the next few sections I will discuss these specific additions rather than a full-blown discussion of XP.

One of the specific development techniques that XP specifies is Pair Programming. This technique has two programmers sitting at one workstation. The person with their hands on the keyboard typing in the code is referred to as the "driver" while the second person is called the "observer" or the "navigator." Working together, the pair implements a specific section of code.

While the driver is obviously responsible for actually typing in the code the observer can help in other ways. From remembering specific API calls to keeping in mind larger strategic coding issues to answering driver questions, the observer is critical for quality code being developed.

It is also important to realize that the driver/observer roles aren't meant to be rigid for a particular development session. If the driver is having a brain lock the observer is free to take over and the roles swapped. Not only does this promote rapid development, but it also can have a mentoring effect when junior and senior developers are paired.

Another specification for XP is Test Driven Development, often referred to as TDD. This means that every piece of functionality developed has an associated unit test written for it.

What is a unit test? A unit test is a small piece of software that exercises the true code being developed. It has known inputs and expected outputs and exists within a section of code that is ran separately. Many frameworks exist today that provide testing and reporting capabilities as separate modules in code.

Test driven development in XP prescribes a specific flow when developing a new feature. Namely the following steps are followed:

- Write a small unit test for desired functionality.
- Run the new test, it will obviously fail.
- Write just enough code to complete the new feature so that it will pass the test.
- Run the unit test to verify the code passes.

Now the feature can be changed to be more robust using the unit test to verify that the basic operation still works. This is known as refactoring and is discussed in detail in its own "Just Enough" series book.

XP also specifies a coding standard be followed, which helps to enforce collective code ownership. There are several coding standards, many specific to a particular language. In addition some languages enforce a standard as part of the syntax of the language. XP doesn't specify which standard be used, only that the team is comfortable with it and all developers follow the standard.

Finally, XP specifies continuous process improvement by doing continuous refactoring and design improvement (supported by unit testing) and continuous code integration by using Continuous Integration tools and techniques. This latter technique, often abbreviated as CI, is also discussed in another "Just Enough" series book. However, the short explanation is that all source code is stored in a source repository. Each time a developer updates code in the repository an automated process builds the entire system and deploys it out for testing.

Kanban

Another popular form of Agile development is Kanban. It is arguably the simplest framework of all in that it only has three specifications:

- Visualize the workflow.
- Limit Work in Process.
- Measure the average work item time.

While this is simple in theory, it can be either equally simple or much more complex in actual practice. This is because the workflow process, the heart of Kanban, can either be very simple or very complex.

Referring back to the Scrum task board in Figure 30, a very simple Kanban-like board is shown as part of the Sprint Task Board. It simply has three columns for "Available", "Working", and "Done" but doesn't have any specification for limiting work in progress.

Figure 31 shows a pure Kanban board that could be used instead of the full Scrum process. The "Backlog" column has all the functionality desired by the customer (Product Owner) and they decide which items move into the "Ready" column. This column has a limit of three so the owner is forced to prioritize the next most important work. When the developers move an item into "In Progress" they are limited to five items overall in the "Development" column. This limit is shared between "In Progress" and "Code Review" in this workflow. This ensures that working code is not only completed but also reviewed before moving to "Integration", which as a limit of five.

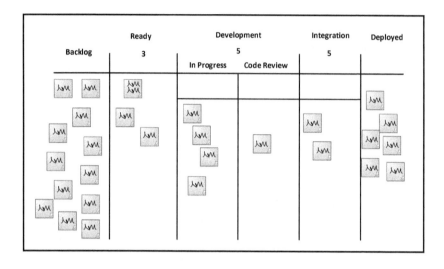

Figure 31 - Kanban Board

The limits in each column are heuristic and may change over time. The effect of the limits is to ensure a smooth workflow and identify and remove bottlenecks. For example, if there are four items in the "Code Review" column and one "In Progress" that is a sign that the development team needs to do some code reviewing before pulling any more items from "Ready". If "Code Review" is full because "Integration" is full then the developers should help with the integration effort.

Also in this flow there is a section at the top that spans "Development" and "Integration". This can thought of as a "Priority Express" lane and may be used for urgent bugs or production issues. Often this lane has a limit of its own, such as one, but it also is held by the overall limit in each column. In this way priority items can be processed and identified in the flow.

In Kanban there are no "Sprints" per se – the work is continuous. In practicality there can many different ways to have a true "release". A more complicated board can be used that has a column such as "Ready for Release". That column can be cleared on a set schedule such as the end of each month or each quarter. There could also be a backlog item for "Release current software" that the owner can pull into "Ready" when they feel there is enough features to release. Any method the team decides on and reliably works can be used – that is the beauty and flexibility of Agile!

Thus far the discussion and illustrations have been centered on "analog" agile techniques. Meaning sticky notes, index cards, white boards, and lots manual writing. While that is the purest and arguably the best way because of the required interaction and visibility, digital tools are increasingly popular especially if teams aren't co-located such that all team members can walk to the task board.

There are many digital tools for both Waterfall and Agile. For the purpose of this discussion I will be using the Jira® suite of Agile tools to demonstrate a Scrum project. There are many others that offer similar capabilities and transferring knowledge shown below to them should be trivial.

For the following discussion I will be referencing a fictitious project known as the "Application Inventory Management System", or "AIMS". The goal of the system is to allow managers to track software applications and their related components such as servers and databases.

First off, let's start with the Product Backlog. Figure 32 shows an initial backlog with estimates. At this point they are in numerical ID order, not priority order. However it can be seen that they have both priorities assigned to them (the arrows on the left) and story point estimates (numbers on the right).

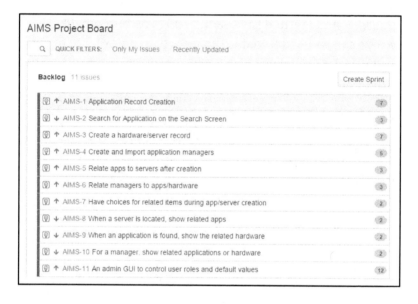

AIMS Project Board

Q QUICK FILTERS: Only My Issues Recently Updated

Backlog 11 issues   Create Sprint

↑ AIMS-1 Application Record Creation   7
↓ AIMS-2 Search for Application on the Search Screen   3
↑ AIMS-3 Create a hardware/server record   7
↑ AIMS-4 Create and Import application managers   5
↑ AIMS-5 Relate apps to servers after creation   3
↑ AIMS-6 Relate managers to apps/hardware   3
↑ AIMS-7 Have choices for related items during app/server creation   2
↓ AIMS-8 When a server is located, show related apps   2
↓ AIMS-9 When an application is found, show the related hardware   2
↓ AIMS-10 For a manager, show related applications or hardware   2
↑ AIMS-11 An admin GUI to control user roles and default values   12

Figure 32 - Initial Product Backlog

If the Development Team has stated that they believe their velocity will be approximately twenty points, then working together with the Product Owner in the Sprint Planning Meeting the items for the first Sprint can be determined. The first Sprint is shown in Figure 33.

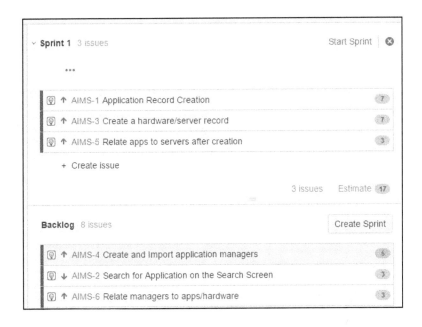

Figure 33 - Sprint 1 Defined

Notice that even though the team has said their velocity is 20 there are only 17 points in the Sprint. The Product Owner could have chosen to put AIMS-2 or -6 in the Sprint, but it is always better to slightly underestimate. If there is extra time towards the end the team can always go back and add one of these items.

The Development Team would create sub-tasks for each story to expand the Sprint Backlog. In Jira these are simply additional items and are assigned new IDs. Once the daily stand-up occurs each of these tasks would be assigned to a developer and then that developer would move them through the various stages in the Task Board. Figure 34 shows the task board after one of the daily meetings.

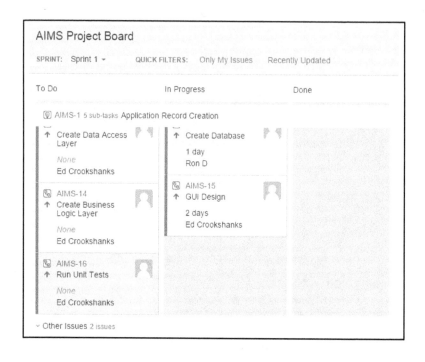

Figure 34 - Task Board with assignments

After each daily scrum, or during the day as the developers complete tasks and pick up other ones, the board will represent the items as they move through the various stages. The board should be public so that all can see, but only the Scrum Master and the Development Team can edit and move tasks. Likewise, everyone should be able to see the Product Backlog, but only the Product Owner should be able to edit and alter it. Online tools enforce this through security roles and it is generally the responsibility of the Scrum Master to set these up.

An example of the task board after a few days of work is shown in Figure 35.

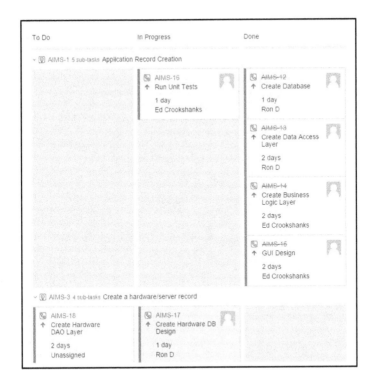

Figure 35 - Task Board after some work

Online applications usually have very nice reporting tools. Depending on how the system is set up it can keep track of story points or time remaining/expended in a nice format. These can be in various graph/chart formats including the normal burndown or burnup charts.

The downside to story points is that if the stories are large or there is a small number per sprint the burndown is not very smooth. This is shown in Figure 36. While the trend can be seen clearly after some stories are complete the task progress during the week is somewhat obscured.

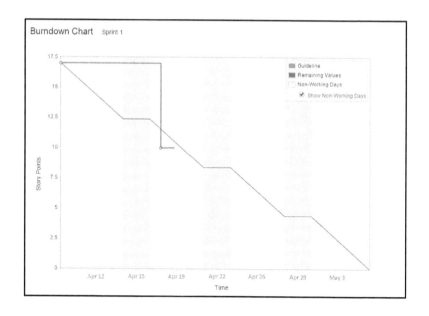

Figure 36 - Burndown chart for Sprint 1

Many systems also allow for tracking hours, however this is usually more work for the team. Each task has to be estimated with a number of hours and during the sprint those hours should be tracked and updated for each task. Despite the work the graph is quite informative and can be displayed as a combination of work completed/work remaining. An example of this is shown in Figure 37.

Another way of reporting is by using the number of tasks. One caveat to this technique is that the tasks should be of similar size. This is potentially easier with mature Scrum teams as they are usually better at breaking down stories into similar sized tasks.

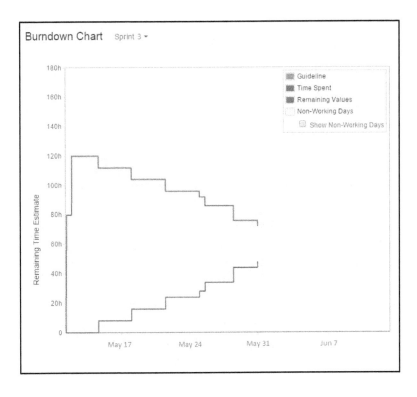

Figure 37 - Burndown/up with hours

Another twist to this technique is that most Agile tools do not allow for simple task tracking. Either points or hours must be used. However, a work around for this can be approximated using an hour-based scheme. The same hour estimate can be assigned to all tasks and this can be updated when complete. This scheme can be as simple or complex as desired. Tasks can have a one hour estimate and be updated as one hour when done. Or tasks could have a four hour estimate and hours could be updated when 25% complete, 50% complete, etc. Using this method an hour-based chart, as in Figure 37, would show tasks complete.

Combining Waterfall and Agile

So far the book has treated Waterfall and Agile as completely separate methodologies for development. Many software organization use one or the other and never combine the two. However some organizations, especially large ones or ones that have had years of entrenched Waterfall development, will not simply drop Waterfall and adopt Agile. Or there may be regulations or programs such as CMMI that are corporate mandated. There is usually a transition period where both are used. Even a permanent combination of the two is used (remember "ScrumButt"?). This section will talk about some possible ways of combining documentation with Agile with the end goal of being completely Agile. In the following sections I will use the Scrum as the methodology of discussion, but Kanban or XP (or something else) could also be used with minimal translation. In some cases I will also specifically point out where one method might have an advantage over the others.

Other than roles and functionality of people, probably the largest conflict between these methodologies is schedule. Agile produces a product incrementally and releases when the Product Owner decides. Waterfall generally has a "big bang" release date scheduled months in advance with the understanding that all requirements in the BRD will be released on that date; any changes must go through the change request process discussed earlier. While there are no foolproof ways to alleviate this discrepancy there two general methods to address it.

One method is for the project manager to create a change request for each and every change along the way. This is process-intensive but may be required for documentation standards. The entire team, including developers, is often tasked with detailing the problem and/or change and this is pure added overhead. While intensive it does have the advantage of producing a solid paper trail and record of all changes, when they happened, and records approval/disapproval for each one. This method may be required by regulation or corporate project control standards thereby giving the project team no choice.

The other method is to keep track of the changes in a "Project Change Log" or similar document and create a single change request before the release of the product. If this type of process is allowed there can be a couple of obvious advantages. One is less CRs and the overhead that comes with preparing them and getting multiple approvals. The other is more practical – a problem that is found early in the development and noted as a change may turn out to be solved be something later. Then it can simply be noted as "solved" and two CRs (one for the original change, one for the fix) are avoided.

The disadvantage to this method is obviously the surprise factor to the end user. It would be the project manager's job to communicate this ongoing log to the users. Unfortunately this is often downplayed as changes mean impact to the functionality, schedule, or both. If the users aren't adequately advised on the change log the release may differ significantly from what they were expecting.

One possible way to combine Waterfall and Agile is to have only the development team use Agile techniques. In this technique the requirements spelled out in the BRD become the basis for the tasks in the Agile process. Depending on how granular the requirements are they may either be stories or tasks. Scrum can then be used by the development team with the caveat that pure Agile flexibility isn't entirely possible; any changes/additions of tasks may require the "outside" project manager to create a change request and follow that process.

The project manager may act as the Product Owner in this scenario. The Scrum Master would assist the Product Owner in translating between the two domains for reporting/tracking purposes. The advantage to this is that if a traditional project manager is involved in this process it may assist in "converting" them to embrace a more agile methodology.

If the requirements are very granular Kanban may actually flow better in this scenario. The requirements would flow directly into the Backlog and the development team would set up a flow to work them through. The project manager could gather progress statistics simply by observing the board.

Another possible way to combine and transition is to have either a small pilot project use Agile, or take an independent component of a larger project and use Agile only on that part. This works best if the team working the Agile project is dedicated to that piece; bouncing back and forth between Agile and a Waterfall project structure is not seamless and could negatively affect both.

Summary

In this book I've discussed and demonstrated traditional requirements documentation along with Waterfall and Agile methodologies. There are many permutations of the format, especially in documentation. The formats shown here can be translated as necessary; regardless of format the terminology is somewhat standardized.

Methodologies are also quite varied in practice. While what has been shown here is a good foundation there are many different adaptions and actual implementation stratagies. Some are even combined such as shown in a book entitled "Scrum and XP from the Trenches" (Kniberg, 2007).

Returning to the aim of the book – the purpose was an introduction to these topics and some practical demonstrations. Having read this book is a start, taking part in an actual project is the only invaluable resource there is!

Bibliography

Beck, K. et all (Web Site) Agile Manifesto
http://agilemanifesto.org/

Kniberg, H. (2007). *Scrum and XP from the Trenches*.
United States: C4 Media.

Schwaber, K. (2004*). Agile Project Management with Scrum*.
Redmond, WA: Microsoft Press.

Schwaber, K. and Sutherland, J. (2016). *The Scrum Guide*.
http://www.scrumguides.org/scrum-guide.html

www.ingramcontent.com/pod-product-compliance
Lightning Source LLC
LaVergne TN
LVHW052307060326
832902LV00021B/3743